101 PET JOKES

by **PHIL HIRSCH**
with **Hope Hirsch**

illustrated by **Tom Eaton**

SCHOLASTIC INC.
New York Toronto London Auckland Sydney

ISBN: 0-590-30380-5

21 20 19 18 17   1/9

Printed in the U.S.A.   01

This book is dedicated to pets everywhere, especially Little Fellah, Rube, Pudding, Gretel, Pepper, Fredo, Clipper, Captain, Pepe, Kippy, Sandy, Frosty, Tinker Bell, Petey Bird, Ferdi, and George . . . not one of whom ever did homework, took a test, failed a class, set an alarm clock, worked, bought a stitch of clothes, mailed a mortgage check, paid taxes, or mowed a lawn!

What Do You Call It?

What do you call a dream in which animals are attacking you?

A bitemare!

What do you call it when 3,000 dogs
and cats get sent to the pound?

A doggone catastrophe!

What do you call a setter who can't
point?

Disa-pointing!

What do you call a cat that likes to dig in the sand?

Sandy Claws!

What do you call it when our feline friends show good manners?

Eti-cat, of course!

What did the cat call it when all the dogs left town?

Good mews!

What do you call a happy Lassie?

A jolly collie!

What do you call a nutty dog in Australia?

A dingo-ling!

Why? Why? Why?

Why did the dog feel as frisky as a puppy?

It got a new leash on life!

O SOLE MEOW...

Why don't cats complain when other cats make noise all night?

Because it's meow-sic to their ears!

Why do some of our canine friends prefer to stay home?

Because it's a dog-eat-dog world out there!

Why do cats sing in back alleys?

Well, that's shoe-business!

Why did the policeman arrest the young cat?

Because of the kitty litter!

Top Dog and Cat Songs —
Ten Great Mewsical Hits!

Pup Goes the Weasel

My Old Kenneltucky Home

The Alley Cat

What's New, Pussycat?

Tommy

Chow Much Do I Love You?

Melan-collie Baby

*Sergeant Purr-per's Lonely
Hearts Club Band*

Purr-sonality

Pet Your Arms Around Me

How Do You...?

How do you stop a 200-pound hamster from charging?

Take away its credit cards!

How do you spell cat backwards?

C-a-t b-a-c-k-w-a-r-d-s!

How do you catch a runaway dog?

Hide behind a tree and make a noise like a bone!

How did our feline friend put the iceman out of business?

Cat got his tong(s)!

How does a horse from Kentucky greet another horse?

With Southern Horsepitality!

What's a good pet for a conceited actor?

A _hamster_!

Can a pet really be worth $500?

Yes, if it saves all its money!

All-Time Furry Favorites

Which is the cats' all-time favorite song?

Three Blind Mice!

What is Dogland's favorite book?

Captain's Cur-ageous!

What is Dogland's favorite TV show?

The (Merv) Griffon Show!

What is the dogs' favorite city?

New Yorkie!

Who was the dogs' all-time favorite comedian?

Growlcho Marx!

Who is the all-time favorite actress among pet lizards!

E-Lizard-beth Taylor!

A-cur-demy Award-winning
Mew-vie Stars

Kat-herine Hepburn

Jane Hounda

Collie Stevens

Mickey Meowse

Fang Sinatra

Bitey Davis

Angora Dickinson

Alfred Hitch-cocker Spaniel

Goldiefish Hawn

Rabbit Redford

LOOK! IT'S MARY TYLER MOO-ER!

Just Jokes

What is the all-time favorite
Broadway musical in Dogland?

My Fair Laddie!

What is another name for a cat's
home?

A scratch pad!

What is the height of bad manners?

Telling a pointer not to point!

What is an important aid in good grooming for pet mice?

Mousewash!

Woof Wit

What dog kisses a lot?

The Greyhound — it's always good for a "buss"!

What dog loves to take bubble baths?

A shampoodle!

What dogs are best for sending telegrams?

Wire-haired terriers, of course!

What terrier is like the little engine that could?

I think, a cairn!

What dog is always good for a laugh?

A Chihua<u>*ha*</u>*!*

Which dog sets a furious pace?

The rushin' (Russian) wolfhound!

Which dog won't do a bit of work?

A "Lhasa" bones!

What dog is disliked by many?

The Doberman, because it's a pinscher!

Pet Puns

Which dogs are made of wool?

Knit-pickenese!

Which dog is as warm as a blanket?

An afghan!

Which dogs speak?

"Herd" dogs!

What dog stands the best chance of winning the heavyweight title?

A boxer, of course!

What kind of dog does Count Dracula prefer?

Any bloodhound!

1st mailman: A dog bit me on the leg this morning!

2nd mailman: Did you put anything on it?

1st mailman: No, he liked it plain!

Purr Time

Why do cats prefer milk?

It's purr-fectly delicious!

Why do most people like cats?

They have pleasing purr-sonalities!

What word best describes the cat
who went through college with an
"A" average?

Purr-fect!

Daffy Definitions

Sourpuss — a cat who likes to eat lemons.

Gigglepuss — what you get when you cross a cat with a hyena.

First-aid kit — a cat who's joined the Red Cross.

Pet Food Foolin'

What do dogs like to eat for breakfast?

Pooched eggs and barcon!

Does a cat have nine lives?

Yes, but sometimes it has Tender Vittles, Friskies, or Puss in Boots!

What kind of sandwich rolls do dogs prefer?

It doesn't matter — as long as they have puppy seeds!

What pet food goes best with milk?

People crackers!

What do you feed your pet frog?

Croakers and milk!

How would you describe, in a word, a dog who hogs all the food?

A pet-a-greed!

Which vegetable is best for your
favorite animal?

Petatoes!

What sign did Mr. Katzen put up
when he opened a hot dog stand?

Katzen Dogs!

What kind of dogs like to eat well?

Chow-hounds!

Pet Store Signs

For a litter of dachshund pups:

Get a long little doggie

For an opossum:

A peticularly good possumbility

For an Angora rabbit:

A rare bit of company

For Siamese kittens:

Take both — they're attached to each other

Just Jokes

Which pets are the most musical?

Trumpets!

Which pets are always found lying around the house?

Carpets!

Which pet is a librarian's best friend?

The <u>cat</u>-alogue!

What's worse than raining cats and dogs?

Hailing taxis!

Which pet snakes do very well in arithmetic?

The adders!

Famous Felines and Distinguished Dogs

Which famous cat never got his feet wet?

Puss in Boots!

Which dog is a member of English royalty?

The Duke of Yorkie!

Who is Catland's heavyweight boxing champ?

Muhammad Ali-cat!

What American statesman is the all-time canine favorite?

Benji-min Franklin!

Who is one cool cat at Christmas?

Santa Claws!

What superhero is Catland's favorite?

Catman, of course!

Top Dog and Cat Movies

The Love Pug

The Gr-r-eat Gatsby

Butch Cassidy and the Sundance Kit

Cur-age of Lassie

Heel-o Dolly

Fangenstein

Cur-eature from the Black Lagoon

The Pet and the Pendulum

The Invisible Manx

The French Poodle Connection

Odds 'n' Ends

Dogs and cats are our most popular pets because:

a. *aardvarks are too nosy.*
b. *you can't fit a hippo through your door.*
c. *it's impossible to walk a pet goldfish on a leash.*
d. *all of the above.*

Jennie: It's really raining cats and dogs!
Janie: I know — I just stepped in a poodle!

Which pet is seen most often on TV?

Rabbit (ears)!

"What's wrong, son?" asks Eddie's father.

"I lost my puppy," sobs Eddie.

"Don't cry," says the concerned father. "We'll get your dog back. We'll put an ad in the paper."

"That won't do any good," wails Eddie. "The dog can't read!"

Pet Places

What country do dogs love to visit?

Mongrolia!

Where do dogs love to go on vacation?

Kenneltucky!

What famous waterway is visited by many dogs?

The Panama Kennel!

What American City is least popular
with our animal friends?

Fleadelphia!

Which dogs come from Spain?

Cocker Spaniards!

Bird-Brained Jokes

What kind of weather excites a pet duck?

Fowl weather, of course!

Which vacation spot will really make your pet bird sing for joy?

The Canary Islands!

What holiday is strictly observed by all birds?

Feather's Day!

How do you stop a 10-pound parrot from talking too much?

Buy a 20-pound pussycat!

Where can birds play professional baseball?

In the mynah leagues!

Pet Puns

What highly valued pet can you find at a dime store?

A goldfish!

What kind of fish can you find in a birdcage?

A perch!

In what state can you find the most little dogs?

In a state of pupulation growth!

What kinds of dogs are full of ticks?

Watch dogs!

When? When? When?

When can you take your pet to a dance?

When it's a bunny hop!

When is a cat biggest in size?

When it's let out!

When is it smallest?

When it's taken in!

When do dogs feel particularly frisky?

When it's <u>leap</u> year!

When is the best time for our cat friends to leave a place?

Anytime it's gone to the dogs!

A brilliant magician was performing on an ocean liner. But every time he did a trick, a talking cat in the audience would scream, "It's a trick. It's not magic. You're a big phony!"

Then one night during a storm, the ship sank while the magician was performing. And who should end up in the same lifeboat together, all alone, but the talking cat and the magician! For three days, they glared at each other, neither one saying a word to the other. Finally the cat sighed and said, "All right, smart-aleck. You and your darn tricks. What did you do with the ship?"

Pet Pitches

What baseball pitcher is a feline favorite?

Tom Seaver, of course!

What Hall of Famer is also popular?

Mickey Mantle, the "soft" paw!

What is the feline's favorite baseball position?

Cat-cher!

Which baseball team do our dog
friends like?

Oh, any ca-nine!

Who is Animal-land's favorite
baseball team?

The New York Pets!

What Did They Say?

What does a cat say when someone pulls its tail?

"Me-<u>ow</u>!"

What did the angry cat say?

"I'm fur-ious!"

What did the angry dog say?

"Them's biting words!"

What did the boy say when he saw his dog lying in the sun?

"Hot dog!"

What did the cat say when it upset the milk dish?

"Nobody's purr-fect!"

What did the pet leopard say after eating its owner?

"That sure hit the spot!"

What did Maw say when she got married?

"Give me Paw."

What do they say about a cat who bites?

"Cat-nip!"

What did everyone ask the angry
butcher when the cat stole
something from his store?

*"What's the matter — cat got your
tongue?"*

What did the salesman say when he
knocked on the door of the doghouse?

*"I'd like to speak to the Mastiff of the
house, please!"*

Just Jokes

Which part of a fish weighs the most?

The scales!

In which branch of military service do fish serve best?

The tank corps!

Who is the superhero of the jungle?

Spidermonkey!

Which heavenly body did the space cat seriously try to avoid?

Sirius, the Dog Star!

Purr-fect Pet Proverbs

Don't put the cat before the horse.

It takes one to show one.

*Early to bed, early to rise, makes a
  manx healthy, wealthy, and wise.*

No mews is good mews.

A stitch in time saves nine lives.

He who laps last laps best.

A rolling bone gathers no moss.

Mice guys finish last.

Tall Tails

Why did the dog keep chasing his tail?

He wanted to see if he could make ends meet!

What kind of turtle can you never trust?

A turtle-tale!

What do you call a gossipy cat or dog?

A tail-bearer!

What kind of a cat writes book after book?

A cat-o-nine "tales"!

Odds 'n' Ends

What did Fido do when he won first prize at the dog show?

He took a bow-wow!

What did I do when a ferocious, 200-pound Persian cat came charging at me?

I-ran!

What did the cat get who played all night under the Christmas tree?

A fir coat!

What do dogs have in common with trees?

Bark!

"Doctor, Doctor, you've got to help my brother! He thinks he's a dog!"

"How long has this been going on?"

"Ever since he was a pup!"

Pet Riddles

What's the difference between Coca-Cola and a cat washing itself?

One is the pause that refreshes; the other refreshes its paws!

What's the difference between a cat and a comma?

One means "pause at the end of a clause"; the other means "claws at the end of paws"!

What animal has the head of a cat, the tail of a cat, and the ways of a cat, but *isn't* a cat?

A kitten!

When is a dog's tail *not* a dog's tail?

When it's a waggin' (a wagon)!

Cat Capers

Can anything be smarter than a cat that can count?

Yes, a spelling bee!

How can you tell if your cat can count?

Ask it what one minus one is, then see if the cat says nothing!

If a fat cat is a *flabby tabby*, what's a very small cat?

An itty bitty kitty!

Which cats love popular music?

Cool cats!

Have you ever seen a

catfish?
catnap?
catnip?
catsup?

Which car do our feline friends like best?

Cat-illacs.

What happens to a young cat who goes on Weight Watchers?

She becomes pussy-willowy!

What food sounds like a bright-eyed, bushy-tailed cat in the morning?

Cats-up!

Last Licks

Where do you find toy poodles?

In a toy store — where else?

Can a cat have puppy love?

Sure, if it's a kitten that's smitten!

Where do dogs like to keep their cars?

In a barking lot!

Can two three-month-old dogs fall for each other?

Sure, but it's puppy love!

THE PUP WAS HERE.
THE PUP WILL BE HERE.
THE PUP IS NOT HERE.

HE'S GOING INTO THE **ARMY**, AND HE HEARD YOU HAVE TO USE **PUP TENSE!**

What is the highest award a cat can earn?

The Purr-litzer Prize!

And a dog's highest award?

The Os-cur!

"Doctor, Doctor, please come over right away. My dog swallowed a fountain pen!"

"I'll be right there, but what are you doing in the meantime?"

"I'm using a pencil!"